SKY NAVIGATION HOMEWARD

First published in 2019 by
The Dedalus Press
13 Moyclare Road
Baldoyle
Dublin D13 K1C2
Ireland

www.**dedaluspress**.com

ISBN 978 1 910251 56 0 hardback
ISBN 978 1 910251 50 8 paperback

Dedalus Press titles are represented in the UK by
Inpress Books, www.inpressbooks.co.uk,
and in North America by Syracuse University Press, Inc.,
www.syracuseuniversitypress.syr.edu.

Cover image © Olga Sinitska – Dreamstime.com

The Dedalus Press receives financial assistance from
The Arts Council / An Chomhairle Ealaíon.

SKY NAVIGATION
HOMEWARD

New and Selected Poems

MIKIRO SASAKI

Translated by
Mitsuko Ohno, Beverley Curran,
& Nobuaki Tochigi

Introduction by Nobuaki Tochigi

DEDALUS PRESS

ACKNOWLEDGEMENTS

The author and translators wish to thank the following people for their support and encouragement:

Nuala Ní Dhomhnaill, Theo Dorgan, Paula Meehan, Pat Boran, Peter Sirr, Cathal Ó Searcaigh, Michael Longley, Ciaran Carson, Mary and Danny Cannon, Mutsuo Takahashi, Willam I. Elliott, Kazuo Kawamura, Marie Heaney, Andrew Fitzsimons, Poetry Ireland and the Yeats Society (Sligo).

Contents

﹏

Introduction

Born in 1947 with a twin brother, Mikiro Sasaki grew up in Osaka, the second largest city in Japan, which is characterized by its commercial prosperity and chatty liberalism. His father, Setsuo Sasaki, was a painter and art teacher at a local high school. Among his former students was Yasumasa Morimura, now an artist of worldwide reputation. Morimura paid tribute to his methodical former teacher, saying that he "devoted himself wholeheartedly and humbly to looking after his students who create works which were beyond the teacher's imagination and lead most mysterious lives". Naturally, Setsuo Sasaki never raised an objection to his son's wish to become a poet.

The work which made Mikiro Sasaki's name well known was an elegy dedicated to his close friend. The pair met in high school in the mid-1960s. The air was politically charged, and they began joining marches to protest against the Vietnam War. On 8 October 1967, Hiroaki Yamazaki aged 18 was killed in a clash between the marchers and the riot police near Haneda Airport in Tokyo. The violent death of Yamazaki, then a freshman at Kyoto University, prompted Sasaki to write an elegy entitled 'Whiplash of the Dead', which became the title of his first book of poems three years later.

Sasaki is a multifaceted poet. After publishing his second collection of poems, he joined a cinema project as a screenwriter. In his thirties, already having gained popularity as a writer, he travelled around rural areas of Japan searching for vanishing oral traditions. He repeatedly trekked in Nepal and Tibet in his forties, and then settled down to dedicate nine years of his fifties to the task of collecting and annotating the complete works of Chuya Nakahara (1907–1937), a great Japanese lyric poet. He and the Japanese poet Mutsuo Takahashi went on a poetry reading tour to Ireland in 1999 and in 2002, became acquainted with Nuala Ní

Dhomhnaill, Theo Dorgan, Paula Meehan, Peter Sirr, Cathal Ó Searcaigh, Michael Longley, and Ciaran Carson, among others.

Sasaki is also known for 'Alice Jam', his experimental project with local people in a place near Mt Asama in central Japan. For more than 30 years, the project members have continued to build cabins by hand in the woodlands at 1300 meters above sea level, and these handmade buildings are now functioning not only as Sasaki's summer house but also as the hub of the local community and a welcoming place for visitors. Such activities have provided Sasaki's poems and prose writings with various topics and motifs.

Sky Navigation Homeward is Sasaki's new and selected poems. The poems were chosen by the poet, most of them taken from four collections of his, published between 1991 and 2011: *Searching for Wild Honey* (1991, recipient of the Takami Jun Prize), *From the Sand* (2001), *Until a Lament is Born* (2001), and *Tomorrow* (2011, recipient of the Hagiwara Sakutaro Award). A few are published here for the first time. 'Procession' stands out as the only poem picked up from his earlier collection *Demented Flute* (1979).

Some readers may have already encountered his poems in the English-language volume, *Demented Flute: Selected Poems 1967–1986* (Dexter, MI: Katydid Books, 1988), translated by William I. Elliott and Kazuo Kawamura. The present volume, being a sequel, encapsulates the features of Sasaki's poems in his mature years.

*

In the following pages, I will try to add some footnotes so that readers can familiarize themselves with the poems in this book.

First of all, let's take a look at 'Procession'. The poem is Sasaki's favourite piece for poetry readings, and he often chants it by imitating the style of a Noh song. His witty performance enticed by the repetition in the text may sound as if it is an incantation that invokes a vision of procession. The poem, however, is not just a ritualistic entertainment. According to Sasaki's recent essay on the death of the aforementioned Hiroaki Yamazaki, 'Procession' was written in 1978, when the poet thought back on his friend's death, which had inspired him to write 'Whiplash of the Dead'. We see now that the poet has been persistently ruminating over the tragic memory.

The reader may find some other poems ritualistic. 'That Voice' has a scent of animism, while 'Roll Out the Barrels' sounds like a work song of the old days, sung in a distillery. These two poems were actually set to music and sung by Hitoshi Komuro, one of the pioneering musicians of the Japanese folk-music revival, at the opening ceremony of the Suntory Museum of Art in Tokyo on 27 May 2007. In the same year, these poems, together with 'A Stone and the Dead' and 'Beginning Begins', were sung and recorded for Komuro's CD entitled *Beginning Begins* (FLCF 4202).

'A Night Prayer' is another poem which has a quality of incantation. By reading the former part of the text aloud, you may even feel as if you are at one with the universe. It is remarkable that the prayer reveals a striking similarity to Douglas Hyde's famous translation of 'The Mystery' from Gaelic. 'The Mystery' is attributed to the Milesian poet Amergin on his first landing to the Irish shore:

> *I am the wind which breathes upon the sea,*
> *I am the wave of the ocean,*
> *I am the murmur of the billows,*
> *I am the ox of the seven combats. . .*
> *I am the God who created in the head the fire. . . .*
> *Who is it who throws light into the meeting on the mountain?*
> *Who announces the ages of the moon?*
> *Who teaches the place where couches the sun?*
> >> *(If not I)*

Compared to the amicable narrator of 'A Night Prayer', Amergin is predominantly commanding, but they share the same sense of blissfulness.

I've asked Sasaki if he was aware of the resonance to the Amergin poem. He said he never was, saying that the prayer was his adaptation, having modeled it after a poem called 'The Delight Song of Tsaoi-talee', which he read in Hisao Kanaseki's Japanese translation. The poem's author is a contemporary Native American poet, N. Scott Momaday. A recipient of the Pulitzer Prize for his novel in 1969, Momaday is much better known as a fiction writer, but 'The Delight Song of Tsaoi-talee' retains a strong connection to the indigenous song tradition. The poem goes:

> *I am a feather on the bright sky*
> *I am the blue horse that runs in the plain*
> *I am the fish that rolls, shining, in the water. . .*
> *You see, I am alive, I am alive*
> *I stand in good relation to the earth*
> *I stand in good relation to the gods*
> *I stand in good relation to all that is beautiful*
> *I stand in good relation to the daughter of Tse-tainte*
> *You see, I am alive, I am alive*

It is fascinating to know that poems sung or written within totally different historical and cultural backgrounds can reverberate with each other in this way.

'A White Chair Burning in the Morning Sun' shows that Sasaki has a great affinity for visual arts, too. The narrator finds himself in a picture when he wakes up, and he declares that he grasps the world in terms of "a circle or a straight line". He was "born to move within this picture / as a cube" and, within the frame free of gravity, he mutters to himself: "Could there be any lighter vessel / befitting my life?" He seems to drift around in a kaleidoscopic space of a Cezanne (or a Dalí, should we say?) painting without knowing where he is headed to.

Sasaki is inclined to obscure the core of things. For example, 'Opossum and Beans' admires the animal that has such a small brain but is an absolute pacifist. The moral which 'Imagine:

sleeping meant fighting for them' carries can be variously drawn, but if you are informed that the poem's first appearance in a journal was in February 2002, opossums can be seen as a desirable metaphor of human beings. The bombing of Afghanistan by the United States and British forces began in October 2001, and the image of sleeping opossums reminds us of those who were holding a "die-in" as a way of protest. A careful reading may uncover what is unsaid in the core of the poem.

'Terraced Fields in the Rain' and 'In the Sleep Forest' are the poet's observations and meditations on his trekking tours in the Himalayas. The image of "Ammonites sleeping on the ground" in the latter is unusual because we think fossils are normally underground, but Sasaki has reported that he has seen a fossil ammonite visibly embedded on the ground in the mountains in Nepal. He wrote in an essay that his interest in Nepal was ignited in 1986, when he saw a photograph of "something which looked like a huge snail squatting on a hill". Two years later he went to Nepal for the first time to see the ammonite fossils on the hills with his own eyes.

'Tree', in turn, tells of a cultural diffusion from China to Japan. The narrator who "had been swept away" was born in a hut specifically built for childbirth in Japan. "[A]n island in the eastern ocean where tall mulberry trees grew" is an epithet used in ancient China to refer to Japan, whereas "nine bronze-faced crows" emblematizes the sun. Mulberry leaves are widely known as silkworms' preferred food and, actually, silkworm culture was introduced to ancient Japan from China together with those emblematic images. "[M]y mother lighting the ocean and the sky" indicates the celestial sun goddess Amaterasu in the Japanese myth, and the "silkworm eyes" can be associated with the Japanese people and their ancient textile industry. "Amah" can mean both the ocean and the sky in Japanese, and "Anmah" means mother in Okinawan Japanese.

'A Tale of the Sand Garden' is a poem dedicated to Nuala Ní Dhomhnaill, in which she appears and says "Mythology // in former days belonged to households". Sasaki and Ní Dhomhnaill have known each other since 1998 when she visited Japan. In the following year, they met again in Dublin to give a poetry reading together. After the event, Ní Dhomhnaill invited Sasaki and his friends to her summer house in Dingle. Sasaki was deeply impressed with her knowledge of local place names and stories embedded in the landscape. The encounter with her words of wisdom induced him to compile fragments of his childhood memories and lay out a garden made of his own words.

Quite a few poems grew out of Sasaki's experiences in Ireland. He made a trip to the Aran Islands on his second poetry reading tour in 2002, and 'Riding the Sea' was written in Japan, looking back on his visit there. In the opening lines, the narrator deftly compares his tired body to the 'drowned body' in Synge's play *Riders to the Sea*. 'Marys and Dannys in the Garden' is a fruit of the poet's visit to Donegal. There is a story behind the poem: Cathal Ó Searcaigh arranged a kitchen session of local musicians at a B&B owned by Mary and Danny Cannon in Gortahork to welcome Sasaki and his friends. After a long and pleasurable night, the poem describes the dewy garden in the following morning. Sasaki was to meet Ó Searcaigh at nine but he did not show up on time. Thus, the last three lines. The poem was set to music and recorded in 2006 for *Inspiration* (R-0730589) by a group of musicians called VOICE SPACE. Kozo Toyota, who played the tin whistle in the CD, is now an exponent of Irish music in Japan, and he placed third in the slow air competition on tin whistle in the Fleadh Cheoil in 2016.

'Dog in the Field' combines a heavenly Irish landscape with a mentor whom the poet met when he was young. In an essay, Sasaki wrote about "[t]he great man" named Shiro Ikeuchi who was his elder by more than a dozen years: "Mr Ikeuchi never wrote anything. He was never seen reading a book. Yet he talked about his own experiences and of an ideal future, which always inspired me".

Sasaki spent his formative years in Kawachi, a region south of Osaka. Kawachi is where a tumulus culture flourished more than 1500 years ago, and the area has a cluster of burial mounds of ancient kings. 'In the Tomb of the Tenth King' is a fantasia made of dense layers of memories. In the lines, the poet's and his twin brother's private myth or their boyhood memories overlap the mythical landscape of a distant past. "[T]he dragon's eyes" were grapes brought overseas from China. "[T]he red bridge", appearing as "the big bridge in Kawachi" in an old song from *Manyo-shu (Collection of Ten Thousand Leaves,* compiled in the 8th century), is said to be the first bridge built in Japan. "[T]he two round mountains" are called Mt Nijozan, literally meaning "twin peaks", and they draw the eastern border of Kawachi.

'Of the Coral Rock God' is another poem telling of the twin brothers. "[T]he wind cave / on the white sand" is Sefa-utaki, and "an island above the horizon beyond the waves" is Kudaka Island in Okinawa. In the native religion of the Ryukyus, Kudaka Island is the most sacred of islands because the creator goddess of the Ryukyus, Amamikiyo, descended there from the heavens. The kings of the Ryukyus made pilgrimages to the island regularly. Sefa-utaki is a sanctuary under a huge cracked rock on the main island. The kings on their way to Kudaka Island made a visit to this place to look from afar to the sacred island off shore. Kudaka Island and Sefa-utaki are still considered most sacred of the sacred places in Okinawa, and the visitors are expected to pay homage to both places.

In 2005, Sasaki's twin brother, a landscape architect, joined an academic investigation of Sefa-utaki for one day. The following morning, he had a stroke and was deprived of "the power of speech and the movement of the left half of his body". In 'Sky Navigation Homeward' the brother appears undergoing rehabilitation.

'Requiem' was written after the Great East Japan Earthquake on 11 March 2011. "Terrible things descend from the sky" refers to radioactive contamination. The meltdown of the nuclear power plant in Fukushima was brought about by enormous tsunamis. Tidal waves struck the seashore one hour after the earthquake, and caused "all things drift deep into the land". 'Tomorrow' was another poem written in the wake of the disaster, which was set to music and has been performed by VOICE SPACE.

*

Let me add a few words about the translators. Mitsuko Ohno, Emeritus Professor, Aichi Shukutoku University, is an internationally esteemed scholar/translator of Irish poetry who has lectured frequently for the Yeats Summer School in Sligo. Her translations include Nuala Ní Dhomhnaill's poems into Japanese and Mutsuo Takahashi's poems with Frank Sewell into English, collected in *On Two Shores,* published by The Dedalus Press in 2006. She organised Sasaki's two poetry reading tours in Ireland. Ohno has long been wishing to translate Mikiro Sasaki's poems for an English audience, and, with the help of her former colleague Beverley Curran, the present translations were finally made possible. Professor Curran has written about Irish, Canadian and Japanese literatures, and she teaches translation studies at the International Christian University in Tokyo.

— Nobuaki Tochigi, Waseda University

はじまり　はじまる

はじまりは　すいせんのはな
はじまりの　めおはしろくて
はじまりの　くびはながくて
はじまりは　ゆれつづけてる

はじまりの　はじめはどろで
はじまりの　かたまりひとつ
はじまりは　しずまりはじめ
はじまりは　もつれはじめて

はじまりが　はじけるときに
はじまりの　ものういあくび
はじまりに　はるかぜふいて
はじまりは　はじらいはじめ

はじまりの　ほほはきいろに
はじまりは　いのちのはじめ
はじまりは　とどろきのなか
はじまりは　いのちのしるし

佐々木幹郎

'Beginning Begins'
handwritten Japanese original by Mikiro Sasaki

A White Chair Burning in the Morning Sun

When I first woke up
in the woods,
I found myself in a woodblock print of Edo chiyogami paper.
Distant tree branches and shrubs were pale grey,
the trunks of the red pine were gleaming.
When I next awaken,
I think everything in this world will be a circle or a straight line.
Beyond the mountain the sky was hollowed out in a semicircle,
outside the door a white chair was blazing up,
the birds were melting in the morning sun,
giving away only sporadic chirps.

Toyama/Door Mountain
Sotoyama/Outside Mountain
Outside the door.
I have
nothing with me,
born to move within this picture
as a cube.
Why is a transparent glass containing rainwater beautiful?
From summer to autumn
watching the green chestnuts grow day by day,
a flame forms inside a boy,
so, for the time being, let's try a walk
like a little sea urchin.

One summer afternoon
I surely saw a one-mast ship
sliding on the bamboo leaves
on the slope of the woods.
A mid-day flame
blazing upon the pilgrimage of the sacred land,
lit by the golden sun through the tree branches.

Who was on the boat?
Portions to be consumed in the flame,
blood splash and sneeze,
soon they will entirely vanish.

When it begins to rain,
leeches that have climbed onto the boy's knee
will walk on his forehead.
Looking down from the dry stone-staircase of the temple
at human bones
and pieces of wood
floating on the waves of fire,
what difference is there between them, I wonder.
The flame destroys everything
by licking away all mortal beings
like a ridiculous cotton candy.

What is blazing up
overtakes what has gone by,
drawing a concentric circle
in a small bay,
past a man remembering the past.
Could there be any lighter vessel
befitting my life?
When sparks fly up from the flaring flame
like sperm sent into the atmosphere,
what has been forgotten
goes flying over the summer mountain.

Toyama/Door mountain
Sotoyama/Outside mountain
Outside the door.
I have
nothing with me,
born to move within this picture
as a cube.

That Voice

That voice comes
from inside a stone
all night through
footfalls of water.

Inside the stone
a ship awaits
the rising of the moon.

Darkness is swelling up
the white sail
billows and rustles.

Fragrant surges the sea swirl
thriving within
that voice.

Stone and the Dead

Losing your tongue. Being silent. Things you can't name.
Letting this one die, killing that one, and hating another.
Where are the words floating? Think.

A stone. Something within the stone, flowing like ancient water.
Making sound. A stone placed on the evening porch.

On the verge of losing words, trying to connect with this world.
Everything is fictitious, but the very illusion spurred them. Like
rice panicles, ripening to burst.

But the dead will come.
Announcing their names they come.
Even if transient names for this world only,
the dead will revive when their names are chanted many times over.
No sooner do the dead revive
than they will pass on.
Together with the horse of Time, they will falter and fall.
The pale horse.
Embracing the firmament upon its side.

But the dead will come.
They come.

For an Unanswerable Question

"There are as many deaths as lives
but death is hard to find,
because dead bodies disappear from the earth."

There are as many lives as deaths
but lives are hard to find,
because the living things are forgotten by the dead.

*

Acacias are blossoming.
Between the hanging white flowers,
dangling clusters of shadow are visible,
and deeper inside are the swollen purple cores.
Behind all these, like a swelling cloud,
rises a song.
Stroking the full term belly,
out crawls tottering
a song.

Beginning Begins

In the beginning is a daffodil flower,
the beginning's face is white,
the beginning's neck is long,
the beginning goes on wavering,

the beginning's origin is mud,
the beginning forms one lump,
the beginning begins to settle,
the beginning begins to tangle,

when the beginning bursts,
the beginning gives a languid yawn,
the beginning is caressed by spring breeze,
the beginning begins to be abashed,

the beginning's cheeks go yellow,
the beginning is the start of life,
the beginning is amid the rumble,
the beginning is the proof of life.

One Word

Say in one word   if you like me or hate me
if you love me   or   not
yes or no   just one word.

When asked   I have never replied
but remained silent   always.
One word   is not the same as a nod
or shaking one's head

one word   is my own language
which needs not be understood by anyone.
It is uttered   and rises like vapour
wetting the wick of a candle   that lights the darkness.

One word   when one loves
one word   when one hates
one word   when one wants to remain silent
one living word   to stay alive.

Roll Out the Barrels
In the Kagura-Uta Song Style

Ya Water from the mountain top
Ya Let it trickle downhill
Ya Over yonder headland
Ya Let us roll out the oak barrels
Ya Fill them up with spirit and relish
Ya Let them age for a thousand years
Ya Peat flavour, saltwater tongue
Ya Roll them fragrant down the glen
Ya Let them roll to where the wind begins
Ya Let them roll up the flaming chest
Ya Feed more fire Kikiririri
Ya Tonight's moon shines here only
Ya Tonight's moon shines here only

NOTE: "Ya" is a Hayashi-word, i.e. a cheering voice in traditional songs, its meaning unknown. Here it is used to mimic the call of encouragement when they roll the whiskey barrels.

"Kikiririri" is a phrase taken from the beginning of a Kagura-uta song 'Kikiriri'. Possibly an ancient Korean word, its meaning unknown. Here it represents the excited voice uttered when the spirit imbues your body with sensation.

Procession

The procession's head
is biting the tail of the procession
the procession's mouth
is chanting the future of the procession
the procession has neither eye nor nose
the procession's robe is melting in the night's darkness
even if the procession's past catches fire
the procession can't contain its fear
the procession's sash won't slacken
the procession's length has no reason
the procession from one end to the other
runs around a monk from the procession
the procession has no voice
in the procession's transparent
centre of the procession
is no terror of the procession,
from one darkness to the other of the procession
glowworms flitter.

Sentiments

In the autumnal town
sentiments are strewn here and there
to bruise you without warning.
Made sad in return,
sentiment sometimes
turns into a metal spoon
and mutely rests on a wooden table.
Yesterday he was sulking at the side of a porcelain plate,
today taken out of a kitchen drawer
he is breaking the half-boiled eggshell in good humour,
now I am leaving for a picnic
and have no time for grieving.
Inside a caged-up heart
look, the little birds are fluttering.
Sentiments are strewn around every town
stark naked till they sing out.

Morning Glory

à la Tragedie Graeci

Where in the world am I running away to?
To what town?
(to the furthest place from this nation)
I shall do as I am told.
(through the paths of stalks)
Where am I going?
(climb to the skies)
Then where?
(to Heaven)
Ah, a sanctuary
But what will protect me there?
(your soul in the shape of a flower would be your guide)
My abundant ivy forming a mound
I will lift my visage to the sunrise
Nevertheless the fact remains I have betrayed my nation
and run away like a coward.
Wherever I go and live
my shame will be apparent.
(but the soul knows no shame)

Love

You whisper in Topka language
I gaze at your fingers,
I talk to you in Ratsure
you gaze at my nose.
A black dog is following us,
Ayeen Ayeen
barking in his dog language.
The mountains remain voiceless in the cloud,
trees rumble
water falls.
A little goat's black tongue
licks my face as I lie on the grass
and softly passes by.
If your eyes meet
white grainy sands remain,
barley's ears are swaying
though I am already tired of words.

An Odd Fruit

A poem hangs in the crevice between order and chaos
but a fruit sits within a stubborn mass.

Whether poor imagination murders words
or poor creativity yields words is unknown.

Are trees always natural and so should be words? The
word 'human being' so detached from nature evokes

no sorrow in a fruit. Only animals can experience sorrow
but within the thick shrubbery of sorrow the fruit ripens.

If a fruit can feel joy, it may be when the seeds fly into air
or does that shout of joy belong to the blowing wind?

The end of the world and the end of my life do not seem
to coincide but they suddenly fall into step in a poem.

Silently I search for words. Not because I don't wish to pass them
but to make sure to pass them on to someone else, I keep silent.

Is a poem like a wife or a lover or a roommate or a neighbour or
     a friend
or an acquaintance or a relation or an abandoned hatchet in the
     woods?

Is a poem really a mere passing pleasure? The trees are swaying
for me alone, and likewise what seems like a poem keeps on
     quivering.

My Honey

An apple was
always painted in the canvas corner.
In the same way in my heart
the same curved shape dwells.
I cannot abandon a single thing
so I let my apple simmer till it turns into jam.
The letter the painter sent me before his parting
had an apple stamped on it.
We placed honey in his coffin
so he would become a honey man and wander in the
    netherworld.
Inside my body lodges
this same sweet maze
of apples, painted and unpainted.
The apple decaying on the windowsill of the artist's studio
accumulates honey in secret and keeps turning on itself.

Feeding the Fire

All things burning are turning,
twisting
upward or else downward
sideways or horizontally,
sliding
deeper into the fire, toward the bottom of the fire,
striving to reach the end, and get incensed.
Transparent death alone can block its way,
or in the ultramarine blue
life, Ooh, water
Oooh, chirping with low voice,
the pain of scorching fire tips, its sweetness,
blood oozing out, flirting,
eating wind.
All things burning are turning.

Night Prayer

I am the grass floating in the sky
I am the rain pattering the grass
I am the rabbit hopping in the rain
I am the craggy rock the rabbit jumps under
I am the moonlight lighting the rock
I am the waterfall dripping and screaming down
I am the glittering fish swimming at the bottom of the waterfall
I am the shadow chasing the fish
I am the setting sun rising from the shadow
I am the glitter of the wetland at the sunset
I am the strongest of the shining stars
I am the chill of the star-dying dawn
I am the powdery snow dancing away in the chill
I am the spring wind blowing down the snow slope
I am a bee flying in the spring breeze
I am the blossom with a bee swarming honey pot
I am the stillness of the bulging blossom
I am the round cry in the stillness.
I and I alone
amid this circular chain of all living creatures
is setting out the boat, and rowing along
like the mountain folk.

There came a long-distance call and I talked for two hours,
mostly mere replies by nodding.
The mirage-like sacred wars, women's riots on the other side of
    the earth,
my friend's recent purchase of a new motorcycle
etc. etc. came to my knowing.
After the phone call closing the eyes I thought I saw
in the depth of my sleepy eyelids a lone cactus

standing alone in the desert
but, no,
it wasn't me.

Opossum and Beans

The dry sounds in the skull are the beans:
25 for an opossum, 35 for a skunk
150 for a raccoon, 198 for a ginger fox
325 for a coyote and 438 for a wolf.

In the snow-covered wasteland of North America
Seton says
opossums are beyond salvation.

A skull, able to contain 25 little beans only,
what thoughts does it have?
If you run into one of them in the woods, it suddenly closes its
    eyes
to sleep for hours, playing possum.

For our ancestors who lived as hunters
these were the first beasts that did not know to fight.
Imagine: sleeping meant fighting for them.

In the Kentucky winter
right next to the oven at Auntie's house
an opossum was asleep
and raised his head and went out to the snowy field.

Seven days later
scratching the kitchen door at night
ten opossums returned.

Auntie tries to think
about the warmth,
about words transmittable to fellow
opossums in the opossum language.

Next to the oven, the ten opossums sleep on.
What does it matter; the size of the skull?
What does it matter; how many beans in the skull?

Terraced Fields in the Rain

You talked about
the people in the rain country in the midst of a long rain.
You talked about how capricious it feels
when the sound of pattering rain turns to a whisper.
You also asked when the rain clouds will go.
So I will tell you about
the mountain of eternal youth and everlasting life.
That's where the rain clouds of the whole world boil up;
the rain country was made
by the spirits dwelling in this mountain.
There under a big rock
is a house with woven bamboo walls,
on its dirt floor is a bright-eyed goat
unafraid of the rite of sacrifice.
Plates are wiped with mud and washed
and a small amount of grain is put on them.
A glacier from 100 million years ago melts
and the water is always fresh.
A fat cat dozes all day long.
When travellers pass by on the village road
they are unaware that this is that mountain.
Village houses are clustered on the mountain top
from the stone roofs smoke rises now and then.
Looking back on the mountain path the traveller is finally aware
there is no one in the village,
nor is there his own travelling body.
Death glittering
scatters from here like pollen,
riding on clouds to be delivered to the whole world
to the terraced fields in the rain
of a faraway rain country at the foot of a mountain.

From the Sand

What you remember begins from the sand
what you can't remember
also begins from the sand.

On your way here, you
turned on the mountain road that reminded you of your
    mother's ears
and heard again and again in the valley the dry wind
that sounded like your father's cough.

Memory is a dead body.
Soon, from there, by the time you are born,
each memory stands out like each grain,
lit by the day's moon, and the night's sun,
and becomes an invisible wind.

Your mother and your father
were born like that,
and you also
were born from this country of sand.

In the Sleep Forest

Sleep in a sleeping bag
Sleep on tree branches
Sleep in the middle of a road
Sleep reclining on a rock.
As sleep continues
man's mind grows brighter
and can substitute for his closed eyes.
Man's fate in broad daylight
is invisible even to gods.
Ammonites sleeping on the ground
dream a billion-year-old dream,
sleeping Buddha in the lotus flower
simply sleeps on,
a pond-skater sleeps on the water's surface,
and looking at his ripples we sleep on.

Tree

When I woke up from the dream
I had been swept away
onto the birth bed.
My mother stretching both arms
to hold on to a tree
was smiling.
When I woke from the dream
without even calling God's name
my mouth was wide open.
On an island in the eastern ocean where tall mulberry trees grew
nine bronze-faced crows
stared at me from the tree branches.
Amah, An-mah,
the ocean was called Amah, the sky was called Amah.
An-mah,
I called out
to my mother lighting the ocean and the sky
on the white sand where the ocean and the sky met,
An-mah!
Her silkworm eyes
for 2000 years
have spewed out invisible silken threads.

A Tale of the Sand Garden

to Nuala Ní Dhomhnaill

In a cobbled alley at night
walking barefoot with a shoe in your right and left hand,
you told me, "Mythology

in former days belonged to households."
My grandma's crimson face
was the result of her putting faggots into the cooking stove every
    morning,
rice gruel boiling up in the iron pan,

the garden for drying kanpyou gourd shavings
the garden for drying fine soumen noodles
in the garden of the two sisters' house a wheel for spinning
    brocade-threads.

"Don't tell anybody,"
I was five and standing naked,
my willie caught by the sisters,
"When spring comes let's go to the mountain."

I learned the word 'spring' for the first time,
wrote 'spring' with a twig in the sand over and over again,
wrote it on the playground of the primary school next door.

What is spring?
A branch of a cherry tree in full bloom on the mountain,
from the branches men jumped down,
the sisters ran away screaming,

then there was winter,
my grandpa came down from the mountain
with the faint fire of the local sake spreading on the tongue at
    midday,

he kept on singing the song for warding off evil spirits,
winter was easy to understand,
utter white
from the top of the cliff the sisters and I watched snow falling on
    the mountain,

other than that
I knew neither summer nor autumn,
perhaps they are the faery boats leaving no trace on the waves,

the heavenly galleons gathered on the top of the mountain,
at the foot of the mountain at the ancient water's edge,
I made an arrowhead with the black andesite
and continued to listen to the cry of the cicada,

at the age of ten I am
a child of summer and autumn,
so I think I know

the grief of the cicada's transparent shell,
to live
is not to pause,
to live is wilful,

like the booze distilled from the spreading fog
over the bogland,
your garden sustains its fragrance,

the sweet smell of the peat glowing in the hearth,
the mythology of your land that stays green all year,

to the sound of the waves in the distance,
you said, "mythology"

the tales of the wilful
gods and of the living garden,
"in former days belonged to households."

Anxiety

Montbretia of the genus Montbretia
of the Iridaceae family; long ago
mouth pouting, escaped
from the Imperial Botanical Gardens in London,
today in Ireland
its orange flowers bloom everywhere.

In a moment
the flowers receded from our view.
As the windows of the bus were fogged
we tourists
turned our heads ahead at once
showing our flower bulb faces.

Having set out from Africa
our ancestors walked
across Eurasia
beyond the Aleutian Islands
to North America and on to South America,
I wonder
if they ever felt lonely,
or our ancestor from a small South Sea island
coming on the Kuroshio current all by himself,
did he on the raft
feel 'lonesome' at all?

Shadows of the flowers still remain in my sight
seeking water even now.
I am wondering as a flower bulb
blooming alone,
am I feeling lonely?

Montbretia of the genus Montbretia
of the Iridaceae family;
In flower language: 'Anxiety'.

Wilderness in the Window

at Yeats Memorial Building, Sligo

Visible from the window
is a red-brick house, our venue for today
and next to it a river of black water,
frothy waves
making brown spray here and there.
People cross the bridge in silence,
a man with a fiddle-case on his shoulder a moment ago
cast an eye on the swans in the stream.

The brick entrance hall is open
but quiet with no visitors,
at the window is a photo of the poet standing in the wilderness
it alone looms up there,
soon I will be within that window
to join the ranks standing in another kind of wilderness.

The brick house listens to the sound of the river.
As the heartbeat runs through my body,
may the passing word, tracing the stone form of the house,
like a rabbit lured out by the wild wind,
become a rabbit.

Marys and Dannys in the Garden

in Gortahork, Co. Donegal, Ireland

The flowers in the garden are the faces of
Marys and Dannys.
Danny shows himself from the foliage of yellow-green hedge;
The stubborn face, a piece of wave-weathered driftwood.

Hydrangeas are the hue of summer ocean.
When you go through the arch of rose branches,
Mary greets you through the flowers of white althaea.

Here and there, blown by the wind, fuchsias
Are ringing their scarlet bells;
While Mary's lily is swinging her little chin
With pink lips.

Next to her, reaching out his verdurous arm,
Is a white daisy, Danny.
Oh, look at the saffron yellow pumpkin chuckling.

On the lawn beyond is a hive, a work of Danny's;
Those pulling out their plump rumps
From the round holes of the wooden house at 7 a.m. sharp,
And then flying and dancing, are countless Marys.

From the west to the east,
The clouds are flying swiftly
Without leaving anything behind.

It is clearing and brightening up
In Gortahork after the shower –
The clouds begin to glitter on the blades of grass.

It is only the garden that is murmuring.

Nobody here in this village keeps
Promise to meet
At 9 a.m.

Translated by Nobuaki Tochigi

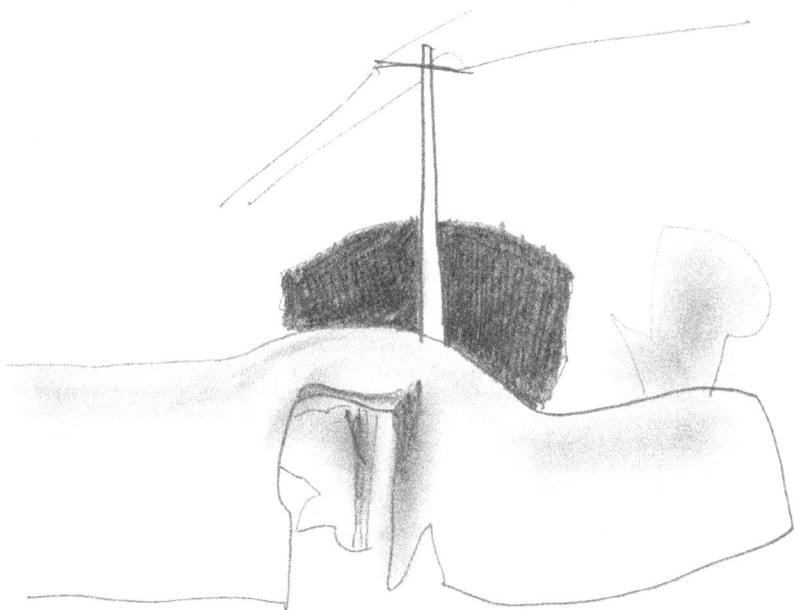

Sketch by Mikiro Sasaki

Riding the Sea

As if pushed back by a big wave
I was in bed this morning,
sweaty, ugly,
facedown, a drowned body.

When the first wave came
it brought a great mass of songs,
when the next wave came
it carried you ashore.

So said the islander
and left me in bed, on the soles of my feet
are rock-hard blisters.

Exhausted from walking on a craggy island,
perhaps it was an illusion
everywhere along the path crimson fuchsia bloomed.

Lamenting and bewailing
small voices multiply
by the shore, off the washed-up body
women ripped the sweater and counted the stitches.

"Four stitches less sixty,
this must be the sweater I have knitted,
so this is none other than my big brother."

A boat
drifts over the sea waves,
Aran in olden days meant an inner organ.

A burning piece of turf
drops off the fireplace,
Aran in olden days meant a human spine.

On the bare craggy island
a clothesline sways in the wind
white shadows of sheets dance like squids.

All I saw was that scene,
the rest was stone walls
and amid the rock-strewn barren field
a stone barrel for storing rainwater.

Walking around I heard for certain
the staring cows' mooing,
and saw the ropes gripping the thatched roof
and the gloom in the house bound with ropes.

I saw the rising sun lapping the seashore
and the blushing sun setting at the sandy peninsula's head,
wrapped up by the island fog
I tried to speak to a puppy.

In the summer morning,
roots of the potatoes, nourished by seaweed
spreading in the thin soil over the rocks
reach out horizontally to grip water.

Like that I want to have
a plaster fireplace,
and the fire tongs one grips

with the thumb and the little finger plus three other fingers
    outstretched.

I also want a burning sod
that drops abruptly from the fireplace
when I get tired of talking.
Then replied the puppy:

Potatoes should be eaten in the smoke,
stripped of its thin purple skin
and crumbling on the plate,
potatoes are best eaten in the whiff of turf smoke.

I climbed up the stone wall
and coughed many a time,
the flourishing flowers in the ancient fort turned into an illusion,
the puppy in the fog barked at me many a time.

An island
drifts over the sea waves;
Aran in olden days meant an inner organ,
Aran in olden days meant a human spine.

Waking up I pared with a knife
the solid blisters off my sole,
walked toward the desk,
and then wrote a poem.

NOTE: Aran Mor is the biggest of the Aran Islands, floating offshore in
the west of Ireland. The epigraph and the quotes are from J. M. Synge's
The Aran Islands and *Riders to the Sea*.

TRANSLATOR'S NOTE: According to W. F. H. Nicolaisen, the Irish name
of the Aran Islands *(Oileáin Árann)* is usually thought to derive from Early

Gaelic *aru* ‹kidney›, due to the kidney-shaped ridge of Inis Mor. Tim Robinson in *Stones of Aran* suggests the same root but a different route; as mentioned by Uri Granta, "The name 'Arainn' ... derives from the word *ara,* a kidney, the sense of which has spread to include the loins and the back in general, and so come to be applied to the back of a rise of land..."

In the Tomb of the Tenth King

a Kawachi vision

At night when beetles gather,
inside the kings' tombs
the two brothers go roaming
looking for their sister
amid the odour of honey, the scent of resin.

Inside the tomb of the first king, a white heron sleeps,
in the second king's tomb is a decoy,
in the third king's tomb, only lotus flowers are floating,
in the fourth king's tomb, water is brimming.

There is a rock with an arrow piercing it
and a path the long-shinned men escaped by.
The pampas grass swaying on the coast,
swept by the wind, reaching the rim of the mountain pond,
stands stark, naked.

You saw, brother, didn't you
you saw the dragon's eyes
so many of them, hanging
from the mountain trees?

If you ate these brought from the sand country
carried in a big ship
and across the red bridge,
if you could only eat them
my rain will also be quelled.

In the fifth king's tomb runs a highway,
in the sixth king's tomb, only opened coffins lie,
nobody knows where the seventh king's tomb is,
the eighth king's tomb is utterly forgotten.

Tapping with rhythm,
identifying by the smells of resin,
the brothers tap only the white tree trunks,
while transparent cicadas flutter inside the brothers' bodies
and falling raindrops turn into cicada wings.

The older brother gets stuck in briar on the shore,
the little brother's feet are caught in the mire,
without making a sound
both of them are crying.

When, between the two round mountains
the sun rises,
the mother claps her hands to pray
the father lights his pipe to smoke.
What a brilliant morning.

From the ninth king's tomb, clouds descend.
Over the tenth king's tomb a ship flies by
carrying their sister away.

Of the Coral Rock God

I suppressed and killed the hushed voice,
someone praying sits at the other side of the wind cave
on the white sand.
The prayer, under the great mass of coral rock
drinking the dripping water out of sight.
On an island above the horizon beyond the waves
white butterflies swarm at the forest entrance.
Once I violated the sacred ban there
and left the island as if to escape
without a word of excuse.

Thirty years later
in front of the wind cave, forgotten memories return.
Were they the countless souls of the dead there, seeking water
floating in front of me?
Charmed by their beauty I stepped into the forest.
Being, not a woman, but a man,
why was it forbidden, why a sin?
Since then many times sitting on the beach
praying to the beach stones and to the waves, I apologized
    to the island.
You could kill me if it was my fault.
I know there were people surrounding me
smiling sinister spine-chilling smiles,
they could have pushed me off the cliff then.
I would fall off the cliff without uttering a cry,
my voice mixed with waves and fading
I told you that, do you remember?

But you did nothing to punish me.
If you must chastise a man who violated the ban
it should be me to be punished over the past years.

But what went wrong?
Why did you misjudge the person?
The one that came here yesterday was not me
but my younger brother,
how could you mistake my brother for me?
Why did you deprive him, though he came solely to admire you,
of the power of speech and the movement of the left half
    of his body?
Well, his speech at least returned with time,
with gratitude I admit it,
and I am grateful too that his hemorrhage was limited.
Yesterday at this cave my brother met you,
it was fantastic, he told me later with his awkward tongue.
But leaving only a white shining stigmata of that impression,
you poured blood into his right brain.
Isn't it unfair?
It was a punishment you should have given me.

I wish humbly to beg for your help now,
please hear and grant me my wish.
No, you are obliged to hear my voice.
Whether from the bottom of the coral rock
or from the glimmering white sky over the wind
    blowing through the cave,
you mistook his identity.
I am no longer afraid
of gazing at you.
Even if all the sea water dyed by the sunset
between the yonder island and myself here, sheds crimson tears,
take my left hand and my left foot
make half my body limp
like the seaweed of your island.
Everything in this world feels soft like the sea,
I know not what supports me,
but does it matter?

What you gave me,
does it exist ahead of me,
or is what I think is ahead
merely a vision?
Something green flies over the waves.
Look here too,
small butterflies are dancing around the coral rock.

When the prayer rises, something falls
forward, plunging down dizzily
in the form of blood.

Sky Navigation Homeward

i SKY NAVIGATION HOMEWARD
—to Joseph Cornell's *Boxes*

Over the blue ocean
following the downward path of many a white tumbling moon
to where Aquila and Cygnus are visible,
tormented by seasickness
your traveling shadow has just crossed the sky.
The night wind flickers and passes.
Is that a starfish?
On a wooden board
an unglazed pipe, a few nails,
undrinkable sea water
seen inside an empty glass.
Did he know what he was doing?
Far from the old home
further from the unreachable home,
my little brother's beloved
summer sky was vivid inside the soap bubbles.
Words turn into a deep sigh
that shifts from right to left in a straight line.
The unreachable home remains afar
and in a rectangular box we end our lives.

ii THE SUMMER OF HALF A CENTURY LATER

A touch can tell
that the forgotten muscle still 'exists' there.
These smiling faces of agata-bearded boys and girls
sunken at the sea bottom vanish with waves.

To remind you that it 'exists'
to deceive your brain, I grip your belly muscles and touch
    your fingertips.
Clasping your hands rosy-coloured from swimming,
I retreat in the water and arch backward.

Hoisting up a transparent battle flag
on a sand mountain and a position
secured beyond, what was it you were drawing
within the lively fortress you were hiding with both hands?

My stronghold here was a cob of corn
cunning and unlikable,
looking down without words
I ate unripe blackcurrants with salt.

The smell of the mountain stream, summer watercress
    in full bloom,
when I held both of your hands (Do they 'exist'?)
yellow sand rolled up over my head
and my eyesight faded at once.

One day we practiced crawling on the river bank,
facedown gazing underwater
at the shallow river bed, feeling the pain of breathing
we each stuck our clam tongues out like sirens.

Now clasping both your hands swimming with the right half of
    your body
I wished to move backward and reach the end of time past,
"Dive deeper in the water,"
do not be afraid, no problem, *daijobu*.

It was the word *daijobu*
that sent the signal, a nurse came running at the sound
    of a fallen cane
in the silent hospital corridor, hugging each other by the shoulders
you and I cried only once, facing the wall.

When your body stumbles upon something miserable
it matters no more even if someone sees it.
You really look like twins, an old woman watching TV
    laughs squinting
and an old man opens his paralyzed mouth.

The pleasure of making someone laugh at you, a smile secures
    imagined 'existence'.
Goggles cutting your tears in the swimming pool,
breathing out chlorine air, you repeat the frightening exercise of
    the one-hand crawl.
The old woman says, "Don't look so scared, it won't help your
    swimming".

To the river of our home
comes a lonesome anticyclone like a cradle.

Eerie Silence

in the forest on Islay, Scotland

In the depths of a small forest on the coast of a northern country
I was taught an expression:
"Eerie silence"
Under the branches of an oak tree
which stood like a silent flame against the sky,
someone whispered softly in my ear.
The one who whispered smelled of water
and, at our feet, the fern leaves
like a kitten's tongue were drinking ditch water.
In the water the oak branches cast black shadows
and calling for a storm swaying and flickering
sang a wordless song
(or so I thought but heard nothing
not even birdsong).
We went deeper into the forest on a wooden bridge,
mounds of green moss were glistening.
Like transparent honey,
quiet music drifted at the bottom of the dim light.
What's that?
It's a chair to stay outside of time.
When I turned around that person
once more so softly
muttered *Eerie Silence.*
Nobody was there but an ancient god
from before we were born, a human face
in the depths of the forest.

Requiem

Men sway
the earth quakes
all things drift deep into the land
collapsing
enclosed
chilled
frozen.
Terrible things descend from the sky
falling and piling up
soak into the soil,
all living things yearning for light
the tips of their lives shivering
halt motionless
cry out for water
and for lamenting voices
the white moon shining bright
rises above the woods.

Now is the time to shed light
passing light and darkness
on the mournful souls of
all living things
all drifting things
all collapsing things
all dissolving things
to sense and gasp to grip
signs of surging renewal
and dedicate them to Mother Earth
again
and again.

Men sway
the earth quakes
all things drift deep into the land
collapsing
enclosed
let us be
allowed
to embrace and kiss
this solid earth.

Dog in the Field

The great man
died and then smiled
in his coffin
looking weary.

I've had enough, so let me sleep fast,
he said.
Doesn't this face seem to say so?
Friends also heard that voice.

The great man
never wrote anything.
When he died,
at his wake we beat a wooden drum for prayer

and beating until the stick broke,
we sang obscene songs together.
Cool, I thought,
his life with no desire to leave his words or trace behind.

The great man
before death told his lover his recollections
and fell off the stairs soon afterward
instantly to climb into his dream cloud.

Below me was a lush green shamrock field,
walking on a narrow path where blackberries ripen dark,
I came across a dog running with a stone in his mouth
and from his mouth he dropped the small stone.

When I threw the stone far the dog chased it,
and returning again

he dropped the stone from his mouth.
At what height is your soul flying?

No significance there
in throwing the stone a hundred times and returning
    a hundred times,
but such a dog lives
beyond the green field.

Our bodies decay fast,
from a clouded berry of blackberries
the decay
starts right away.

Writing poetry in order to leave one's trace in the world
will not do, he said.
When you die,
at what height would your soul wish to fly? –

thirty years ago in a log cabin near a large bay
the great man asked me.
Outside was the moonlight, and a shabby alleyway.
At the height of these eaves,

I replied and he said
it will not do. Lower still,
a soul after death glitters azure
and flies breast high, you see.

The great man
smiled after death
in his coffin,
looking weary,

I've had enough, so let me sleep fast,
he said.

Tomorrow

Tomorrow
a different smell than usual
tomorrow
cyclamens are blooming in pink
tomorrow
we will drink radioactive water rained from heaven
tomorrow
even when the earth quakes, gets cold, then freezes
tomorrow
we will still be alive
tomorrow
even if the coagulated terror makes a bottomless cask of us
tomorrow
on the quaking and splitting earth
tomorrow
like flowers we will suck up poison from the soil
tomorrow
even if everything is lost
tomorrow
tulips will let their muddy green leaves bulge
tomorrow
and open their buds all at once in red, yellow and white
tomorrow
with a smile on our faces we will live
tomorrow
wishing to meet someone somewhere
tomorrow
we will plant sunflower seeds
tomorrow
open the curtains on the window as usual
tomorrow
to fill the room with sunshine

tomorrow
we will live on the earth as usual
tomorrow
when we wake
tomorrow